THE BODY BANDITS

Designed by Bill Foster of Albarella & Associates, Inc.

Distributed to schools and libraries
in Canada by
SAUNDERS BOOK CO.
Collingwood, Ontario, Canada L9Y 3Z7
(800) 461-9120

Library of Congress Cataloging-in-Publication Data

Perry, Susan, 1950-
The body bandits / Susan Perry
p. cm.
Summary: Identifies the four food ingredients that
should be avoided, sugar, fat, salt, and nasty additives,
and discusses why foods containing too much of them
are bad for you.
ISBN 0-89565-875-5
1. Nutrition — Juvenile literature. [1. Nutrition.]
I. Title.
QP141.P44   1992
613.2'8 — dc20   91-44939
                                                          CIP
                                                          AC

THE BODY BANDITS

Written by Susan Perry

Illustrated by Anastasia Mitchell

THE CHILD'S WORLD

Do you ever think about the foods you eat? And about what they do once they get inside your body?

If you don't, you should. Because what you eat affects how you feel and look and act.

Many foods do good things for you. They give you energy. They help you to grow and be happy. But other foods aren't as nice. They can rob you of your energy and keep you from looking and feeling your best.

How can you tell which foods to eat and which ones to avoid? By learning to spot a gang of food ingredients called the Body Bandits. This gang has four members: **Shifty Sugar, Foxy Fats, Sly Salt, and Nasty Additives.**

Any one of them can turn nutritious food into junk food faster than you can say "chocolate malt."

The Body Bandits are a sneaky bunch. They hide in all sorts of foods and use lots of false names, or aliases. You've got to be on your toes to catch them.

This book will teach you how to track down the Body Bandits. It will explain how each of them steals your energy and keeps you from being your healthiest, happiest self. It will tell you how to stay away from foods that are bad for you and choose ones that are good for you instead.

But before we get started on the trail of the Body Bandits, let's take a few minutes and imagine you're at a restaurant.

A new restaurant has just opened in your neighborhood. A sign on the door says:

You walk inside and sit down at a table near the window. There's a menu on your table that reads:

Le Menu

MAIN COURSE - pick one:
Big, Fat Hot Dog   Thick, Juicy Steak
Skinless Chicken   Fast-Fried Burger

SIDE DISH — pick one:
Pile of Potatoe Chips   French Fries
Heap of Mashed Potatoes
Slice of White Bread with globs
of butter

VEGETABLE - pick one:
CRISPY, Fresh Vegetables
Mushy, Canned Vegetables
No Vegetable

BEVERAGE- pick one:
Fizzy Soda Pop   Glass of 2% Milk
Glass of Whole Milk

DESSERT- pick one:
Strawberry Pie with whipped topping
Wiggly Strawberry Gelatin
Bowl of fresh Strawberries

Remember: there are no grownups around, so you can eat anything you want.

Which foods would you choose?

Do you think that some of them might be hideouts for Body Bandits? Which ones?

Let's find out more about the Body Bandits right now. When you're finished reading this book, look back at the menu to see if you'd change your order.

SHIFTY SUGAR

Shifty Sugar is the most famous Body Bandit. That's because everyone eats so much of it — about 90 pounds a year.

There's a little bit of natural sugar in fruits and vegetables. That's okay. But most of the sugar we eat is refined, or not natural. It's made from sugar cane and sugar beets.

Where can you find refined sugar? Start by looking in your sugar bowl. It's also added to candy, soft drinks, cakes, ice cream, and breakfast cereals, to name a few. You can't see it, but it's there.

What makes sugar a Body Bandit? To begin with, it's an "empty" food. That means there's nothing in it to help you look or feel good. Just things that can make you fat.

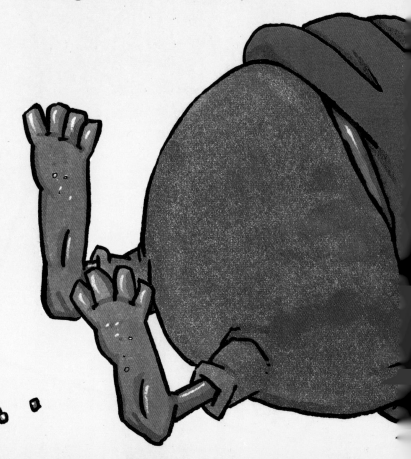

Your body digests it very quickly. It doesn't stay in your stomach long, so you get hungry again fast. And if you eat more sugar to fill yourself up, you end up putting on extra weight.

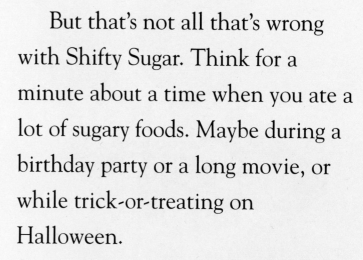

But that's not all that's wrong with Shifty Sugar. Think for a minute about a time when you ate a lot of sugary foods. Maybe during a birthday party or a long movie, or while trick-or-treating on Halloween.

Do you remember feeling tired or grumpy about an hour later? That happened because the sugar gave you a sudden rush of energy. Just as quickly, that energy was used up and you were left feeling blah. You had a "sugar crash."

Professional athletes know about sugar crashes. That's why you won't catch any of them eating a candy bar or guzzling a sugary soft drink before a big game or sporting event. They don't want to be up one moment and down the next. To perform well, they need a steady stream of energy — the kind of energy that comes from foods without refined sugar in them. Foods like fruits and vegetables.

Sugar has one more big fault. It can rot your teeth. The bacteria that live in your mouth eat sugar and produce an acid that gnaws away at your tooth enamel. That's how cavities start.

If you want to cut down on cavities (and trips to the dentist), cut down on the sugar you eat. And brush your teeth — or at least rinse your mouth with water — after every meal or snack.

How can you avoid Shifty Sugar? First, you'll have to learn how to read a food label.

Every can, box, bag, or bottle of food has a list of ingredients printed on it. (It's usually in very small letters, so you may have to look hard to see it.) That list tells you what's in the food inside the package.

You won't always find the word "sugar" printed on the list, though. Not even for foods you know are sweet. That's because sugar has a lot of aliases. Like "corn syrup," "corn sweetener," "honey," "sorghum," "dextrin," "nutritive sweetener," and a bunch of words ending in "-ose" – "sucrose," "lactose," "levulose," "maltose," "dextrose," and "fructose." If you see any of these words on a food label, remember that they're all aliases for sugar.

How can you tell how much sugar a food contains? By the order the ingredients are listed in: The first ingredient listed is present in the greatest amount. If the first word on the list is sugar (or any of its aliases), watch out!

Once you know how to read food labels, you can start eating less of this Body Bandit. Giving it up all at once can be hard. Your body can get used to sugar and think it needs it to be happy.

Some people get bad headaches when they stop eating sugar. It's better to cut down slowly and give your body time to adjust. Try cutting out one sugary food this week, another next week, and so on. It won't be long before foods that contain natural sugars – like fruits – taste sweeter to you, and you won't miss refined sugar as much.

A good place to start cutting back on sugar is with soft drinks. You probably don't know it, but there are eight teaspoons of sugar in an average eight-ounce can of pop.

How many cans of soda do you usually drink every day? Multiply that number by eight to find out how many teaspoons of sugar that comes to.

FOXY FATS

You have to keep a lookout for fats or you'll get fat. Foods that have a lot of fats in them contain more energy, or calories, ounce for ounce than any other food. If you don't burn off those calories by walking, swimming, or exercising in some other way, they'll stay on in your body as extra pounds. And carrying extra pounds around can be unhealthy.

Some scientists believe that fats are Body Bandits for still another reason. They think that fats get together to create a time bomb in the body that can explode years later in the form of heart disease, high blood pressure, or even cancer.

But fats aren't all bad. They help some important vitamins travel through your body. They make your skin soft and flexible. The fat stored in your body cushions some of your internal organs, like your kidneys, and protects them from shock or injury. And the fat that's stored under your skin keeps your body warm.

The secret is to avoid eating too many fatty foods. Milk, cheese, meats, nuts, avocados, olives, oils, and chicken and turkey skins contain a lot of fats. And fats are added to foods like cakes, cookies, sauces, and salad dressings. Some foods, like french fries and potato chips, are cooked in fats. That's why they're so greasy.

In fact, grease is a dead giveaway for this Body Bandit. Sometimes you can see it. Sometimes you can feel it. (Try running your fingers over a slice of bologna.)

Like Shifty Sugar, Foxy Fats can hide behind aliases on food labels. "Shortening," "margarine," "lard," "hydrogenated vegetable (or salad) oil," "coconut oil," and "corn oil" are just a few of the names these Body Bandits go by.

WAIT JUST ONE MINUTE! WHO ARE YOU CALLING LARD?

Cutting back on fats can be easy. Here are a few suggestions:

• Drink skim milk or 2% milk instead of whole milk.

• Once in a while, eat beans or cottage cheese instead of meat.

• Give up hot dogs and bologna – they're very fatty.

• Cut the fat off of steaks and the skin off of chicken and turkey meat before you eat them.

What if you just can't stay away from fatty foods? Well, you'd better plan on getting a lot of exercise – or getting fat!

SLY SALT

Most of us eat far too much of this Body Bandit. We sprinkle it on almost everything we prepare at home, from salads to stews.

But even if we threw our salt shakers away, we'd still end up eating a lot of salt. That's because it's hidden in many of the foods we buy in the supermarket. For instance, cheeses, canned soups, breakfast cereals, hot dogs, crackers, frozen TV dinners, potato chips, pretzels, sausages, ketchup, soy sauce, canned fish, and olives.

Food served in restaurants also contains a great deal of salt. Did you know that the average fast-food hamburger has two teaspoons of salt cooked into it before it ever reaches your plate?

Some scientists think that eating too much salt can cause high blood pressure. This in turn can cause heart disease.

What can you do to stay healthy? Try cutting down on the amount of salt you eat. Taste your food before you sprinkle salt on it – you may discover that it's just fine the way it is.

And be sure to read labels. Like Shifty Sugar and Foxy Fats, Sly Salt has some fancy aliases. "Soda," "sodium," and the chemical symbol "Na" are a few of the most popular ones.

NASTY ADDITIVES

An additive is anything that's added to a food before it's put into a package. There are about three thousand different food additives around today. Some add color, like the caramel coloring used to make white bread look brown. Some add flavor, like the fake "strawberry" and "lemon" flavorings in candy or puddings. Some add texture, like the softness in marshmallows or the creaminess in ice cream. Some, called preservatives, keep foods from spoiling.

I THINK I'LL HAVE FRESH FRUIT INSTEAD!

Food manufacturers use additives to make foods look and feel better. But they don't make the foods better for you. (And they don't make you look and feel better!) For example, artificial colors are used instead of real fruit juice in many soft drinks and other foods. They're cheaper for the manufacturer – but they're not as healthy for you.

Many additives are harmless, like the carotene that adds color and vitamins to margarine. But others may hurt you in the long run. Some doctors think additives may make young people especially nervous. And some additives – like dyes and artificial sweeteners – may even cause cancer.

GRRR!

SNORT! SNORT!

Until scientists know more about these Body Bandits, your best bet is to avoid them. A very long word on a food label probably means there is an additive in it. Some abbreviations do, too. "BHT" and "BHA" are common aliases for preservatives.

Look for packages that say "no preservatives" or "no artificial colors or flavors." Or stick to natural foods – fruits, vegetables, and grains. Eat real fresh foods. If a package claims that a food will be "fresh" for months, it's probably loaded with additives!

THE ROUNDUP

Now you know about the Body Bandits and where their favorite hideouts are. It's up to you to keep them from sneaking into your body and stealing your energy!

What can you do? Catch them before they catch you! Start on food packages. Look for aliases. Work on changing your eating habits. This doesn't mean that you shouldn't ever eat a candy bar or drink a can of pop again, or that you can't munch on a hot dog during a baseball game. Just be sure to eat plenty of good foods. Foods that keep you strong and healthy. Foods that aren't full of those ornery Body Bandits! You'll be surprised at how much better you look and feel.

Remember the restaurant you imagined you visited at the beginning of this book? Look back at the menu for a minute.

Which foods are really hideouts for Body Bandits?

If you were sitting in that restaurant now, which foods would **you** choose to eat?

FOR KIDS ONLY! AND THEIR PETS! No GROWN-UPS ALLOWED